St. Michael's Church, Troedyraur, despite
has an impressive number of tombs and m
conformist ministers. So, to me, St. Micha
various disciplines of the Christian church
am – the strong Anglican influence of my East Anglian forebears, and
the enormous importance of the Welsh Calvinistic Church that has crept
into the Welsh side of my heritage.

This book is dedicated to St. Michael's Church and to the people who
worship there.

All profits made from the sale of this book will be donated to
'The Friends of St. Michael's, Troedyraur, to assist in its maintenance
and restoration.

ISBN 978-0-9563592-0-9

Printed & Bound @
Gomer Press, Llandysul, Ceredigion in Wales SA44 4JL

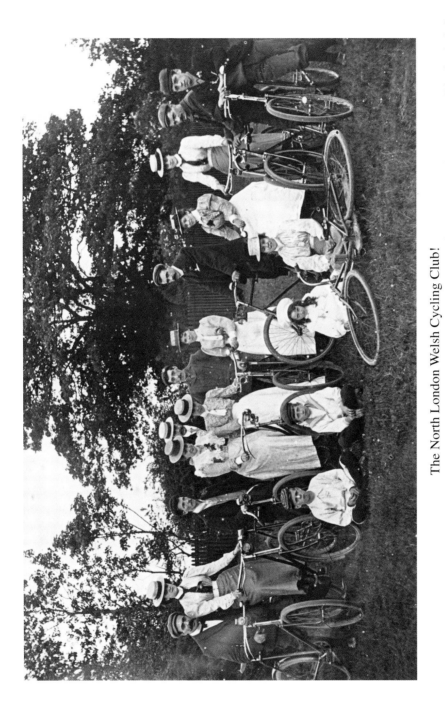

The North London Welsh Cycling Club!

?,?, David Davies, Louisa Morgan, Frederick Chappell, Elizabeth Morgan, ?, Annie Morgan, John Morgan, Lizzie, ?, ?, ?
Front Row, ?, ?, ?, Dilys Morgan

"You must love cooking" is a question that I am frequently asked. I do not, actually, but, I do love feeding people - and there is a very considerable difference in the two statements! I get great pleasure in serving food, and an even greater pleasure in watching how my audience enjoy their food.

My entire professional life has been in management, in the catering and residential industry, and, for the last twenty four years, I have been self-employed, running a guest house, first in Tintern, Monmouthshire, and then, for the last ten years, in Rhydlewis, Ceredigion. My guests often ask me for recipes, and, unlike many cooks, I have no problem in sharing my secrets. But, I think I am now ready to share them with a wider public! The fact that the parish church , (Rhydlewis is in the parish of St. Michael's Troedyraur), needs an enormous amount of money to effect repairs has been the impetus that I needed to put pen to paper.

But what has brought me to live in West Wales? Well, the explanation gives me the opportunity to explain an additional purpose for writing this book! Many of my recipes have been handed on to me by my relatives - I come from a family of excellent cooks, and, in fact, my paternal grandmother was a cook by profession- and I have wanted to record these recipes for future generations. Another of my interests is genealogy, and as I have also gleaned many anecdotes from relatives, I thought that a book would be a novel way of combining both! Originally, the book was to be just for the family, but the need to raise funds for St. Michaels means that the wider public get to share these stories as well - whether they like it or not!! So, why West Wales? My maternal grandmother was from Cardiganshire, and this is where I feel most at home!

Living where I do, I have been overwhelmed by the incredible choice of locally produced food that is available. And it is not hugely expensive either, when bought from the local trades people. Over the years, I find that my attitude towards preparing food has changed. I prefer to cook more simply, and have learnt not to rely on spices and seasonings for

6

flavour. If you have a good, fresh product, the flavour speaks for itself. I have also found that many of my guests also prefer simpler dishes, especially meals that hark back to the 'good old days' when mother had more time to prepare things. Actually, you do not need a lot of time to make these old- fashioned dishes, you just need to be organised!

I had an elderly aunt (affectionately known as Drainpipe Jessie - to distinguish her from another Aunt Jessie- because she always drew pictures of houses for children that had drainpipes on them - funny the things that stick in a child's mind!) Lunch with her was a joy – pork sausages from her village butcher, potatoes and peas from her garden, followed by home grown raspberries (she was still gardening in her late 80s.) Such simplicity, such flavours, such luxury. It was Jessie who informed me that her great Grandfather had been a Bow Street Runner, and indeed, he was – a member of the Mounted Horse Patrol, no less. It was the proving the correctness of this story that has taught me that more often than not, there is a grain of truth in stories that are handed down. Read on…

WEIGHTS AND MEASURES

I make no apology for using the old system of weights, etc. But, making allowances for the younger reader, I have given you the alternatives!!

1 ounce (oz.)=	28 grams			¼ pint (pt.)	=	150ml	
2	"	=	57 "	½ "	=	275ml	
3	"	=	85 "	¾ "	=	425ml	
4	"	=	113 "	1 "	=	575ml	
5	"	=	142 "				
6	"	=	170 "				
7	"	=	198 "				
8	"	=	226 "	= ½ pound (lb.)			
12	"	=	340 "	= ¾ pound			
16	"	=	456 "	= 1pound (lb.)			

OVEN TEMPERATURES

	Farenheit	Centigrade	Gas Mark
Cool	225	110	¼
	250	130	½
	275	140	1
	300	150	2
Medium	325	170	3
	250	180	4
Hot	375	190	5
	400	200	6
Very Hot	425	220	7
	450	230	8

IN THE

BEGINNING…

ANGLESEY EGGS - but as a starter (4)

Traditionally, Anglesea Eggs (Wyau Mon), is a dish topped with mashed potato, and served as a meal. Omit the potato and you have an excellent first course.

Chop a washed leek, finely, and put into a pyrex bowl with 1/2oz butter. Cover and cook for a minute or two in the microwave.
Meanwhile, grease 4 ramekin dishes.
Divide the leeks amongst the dishes, creating a nest.
Break an egg into the centre of each nest, and season with salt and pepper.
Carefully cover with double cream, and sprinkle with grated cheese (Welsh, of course!)

Put the dishes into a baking tray holding ½" boiling water.
Bake in a hot oven at 200 degrees C., for about 10-15 minutes, until the egg white is set.

AVOCADO WITH BLUE CHEESE AND WALNUTS(4)

Mix together 1 tablespoon each of mayonnaise, whipped cream and yoghurt. Add ½ teaspoon of mild curry powder, and a handful of chopped walnuts.

Now add 2oz chopped blue cheese (I use the excellent, local ,Perl Las) and 1 finely diced eating apple.

Cut 2 avocados in half and remove the stone. Carefully remove the flesh, and dice. Mix into the cheese mixture.

Pile back into the avocado skin halves and garnish.

AVOCADO PEAR WITH FRESH PEAR (4)

One of my students, at Parnham House, introduced me to this dish. It's lovely!

Peel a fresh pear and an avocado pear, and cut each into very thin slices.
Arrange on a serving plate and sprinkle with vinaigrette to which a squeeze of lemon juice has been added.
Garnish.

That's it! But you can add a small amount of chopped walnuts if you wish, for a change.

SMOKED CHICKEN WITH MANGO MAYONNAISE(2)

We are so fortunate living in West Wales, to have access to locally produced smoked chicken breasts.

1 chicken breast should serve 2 people.

Slice the breast very thinly, horizontally, and arrange on a plate interleaved with thinly sliced mango.

Add a tablespoon of mayonnaise to ½ tablespoon of mango chutney. Mix well and place on the side of the plate, along with a teaspoonful of neat mango chutney.

Garnish.

BAKED GRAPEFRUIT WITH PORT (2)

Those old enough will remember that this dish was a regular at dinner parties in the 1960s! I still serve it!

Slice a grapefruit in half. Loosen the flesh, removing the hard bits and pips, so that it is easy to eat.
Put into an ovenproof dish.
Pour 1 tablespoon red port over each half, plus 1 heaped teaspoon Demerara sugar.

Pop into a hot oven for 5-10 minutes, and serve.

Try not to burn your tongue!

TOMATO, CUCUMBER & MELON COCKTAIL (4)

I have been serving this dish for years, and goodness knows where I found the recipe. It's a lovely, light dish, as it doesn't compromise your appetite before you get down to the serious stuff! Perfect for hot summer evenings, when you get them.

De-skin 3 tomatoes. Cut in half and remove the pulp and seeds. Slice into slivers.
Peel 4" (about 8cm.), cucumber, and cut the flesh off the middle seeds, which you can throw away. Cut the flesh into small cubes.
Peel ¼ small melon. De-seed, and also cut the flesh into cubes.

Sprinkle on finely chopped fresh mint, and black pepper. Add vinaigrette.

Stir around to mix.

Chill and serve.

STOCK

How many of us have the time to make our own stock? I confess that I resort to bought bouillon, but have never been really happy with the results until I discovered 'Marigold' Swiss Vegetable Bouillon powder. The product is not the cheapest you can find, but I think that the results more than justify the cost! You can get a low salt variety, but I prefer the ordinary 'orange' capped one, but never add extra salt to the dish that I am cooking, as I feel it is salt enough.

A teaspoon of 'Marigold', added to the gravy, will also enhance its flavour.

LOVAGE SOUP

Such a useful herb to grow, but allow plenty of room as it can reach a statuesque 6ft in height.
One or two leaves, chopped and added to a salad lends a lovely celery flavour.

Heat 1oz of butter and sweat off 2 large, chopped onions, and after 5 minutes, add 5 level teaspoons of chopped, fresh lovage (it is a strong and pungent herb.)

After a further 5 minutes, add 1oz. plain flour, and slowly add 1 pint of stock and ½ pint milk.

Simmer gently, remembering to stir, to prevent sticking, for 20 minutes.

Puree, correct the seasoning and serve.

WATERCRESS SOUP

Prepare exactly as for lovage soup, but substitute the lovage with a bunch of chopped watercress.

LEEK AND POTATO SOUP

4 large leeks, well washed and roughly chopped.
Melt 2oz. Butter, and sweat off the leeks for 10 minutes, stirring to prevent browning.

Meanwhile, partly cook 2 large, peeled potatoes (cut into quarters) in the microwave. Crush, and add to the leeks.

Add 1 litre of stock. Cook for a further 10 minutes, puree and correct the seasoning.

COURGETTE SOUP

"French Catherine", as she is affectionately known in Rhydlewis, first told me about
Courgette Soup, and this is my version. When the courgettes are producing fast
and furiously, one can be hard pushed to know how to use them up. As a vegetable,
courgettes do not freeze, but as soup, they do!
I grow, and prefer, to use yellow courgettes, as they produce a beautiful looking
soup, the colour of sweet corn! The flavour is mild and subtle. If yellow ones are not
available, you can use green ones - the taste is the same!

Chop 2 medium onions and sweat in 4oz butter.

Add 8 large, roughly chopped courgettes, plus black pepper to taste.

Cover, and sweat very gently for 15 minutes, so that they begin to produce their own
liquor, stirring regularly.

Add 1 litre stock, and cook for a further 10 minutes.

Puree.

When serving, you can add a blob of crème fraiche or double cream.

WILD GARLIC BUTTER

One of the many joys of the early summer is the smell of wild garlic - or Ramson as it
is known.

Chop 12-20 ramson leaves roughly, and blend with 4oz butter.

This will freeze if necessary.

Excellent used for garlic bread.

THE

SERIOUS

STUFF

DUCK BREASTS WITH SEVERAL SAUCES

Duck breasts are a really useful thing to keep in the freezer. I know that they are expensive, but it's a great treat.

Place the duck breasts in a baking tray, Pour about ½" deep of orange juice (bought juice is fine) around the duck, and roast in the oven for as long as you desire. The fashion is for pink duck, but I prefer to have it well cooked. Prick with a fork until the juices run clear.

Serve with any of the sauces below.

1. St. Clements Sauce: Saute 1 small, finely chopped onion in 1 oz. Butter
until soft. Add 3 tablespoons lemon marmalade, and cook gently until the marmalade begins to soften. Add the grated rind of 1 lemon , ¼ pint orange juice, 1 teaspoon white wine vinegar and 1 teaspoon brown sugar.
Slake 1 dessert spoonful of corn flour with a little orange juice, and thicken the sauce. Correct the consistency.
This, and the other sauces, reheats really well, so you can make it earlier if that helps!

2. Red Fruit Sauce: Saute 1 small, finely chopped onion in 1 oz butter until
soft. Add 2 good handfuls of blackcurrants, or 2 good tablespoons red fruit jam (even the ubiquitous black cherry jam!), ¼ pint red wine and water, 1 teaspoon red wine vinegar and 1 teaspoon brown sugar. Cook gently (if using the fresh black currants, make sure that they are cooked through), and serve.

3. Gooseberry and Cider Sauce: Saute 1 small, finely chopped onion in
1 oz butter until soft. Add 2 handfuls of fresh gooseberries that have been topped and tailed, and cover with cider. Cook gently until the fruit is soft, for about 10 minutes. Add 1 teaspoon white wine vinegar and 1 teaspoon brown sugar, and liquidize. Correct the consistency with more cider if necessary.

MACKEREL WITH GOOSEBERRY SAUCE

Fried, grilled or barbecued mackerel is really good with the Gooseberry and Cider Sauce, given above.

A GOOSEBERRY HINT

My gooseberry bushes are very prolific, so I have to freeze a lot. I have neither the time, or inclination, to top and tail all of them before freezing, so just box them up as they are, in 8oz or 1lb quantities. When I am ready to use them, I flick the tops and tails off with my thumb, whilst they are still frozen.

PORK CUTLET PARCELS

Take a 12" square of tin foil.
Place on it a pork cutlet.
Cover this with fried onions and a layer of sliced apple.
Sprinkle with 2 teaspoons of Demerara sugar.
Seal up the foil parcel.
Place in a baking tray, in 1" water.
Cook in a slow oven , 160degrees C, for about 1 ½ hours.

BARBECUE SAUCE FOR LAMB CHOPS

4 Loin lamb chops
1 tablespoon brown sugar   1 tablespoon vinegar
½ teaspoon salt   ½ teaspoon paprika
1 tablespoon Worcester Sauce   1 tablespoon tomato puree
¼ pint water   2 tablespoons lemon juice
1 medium onion, chopped   ½ oz. Butter
1 stalk of celery

Place chops in a wide casserole and bake uncovered at 200degrees C, for 20 minutes.
Drain off the fat.
Blend the sugar, mustard, salt and paprika with the tomato puree and liquid ingredients.
Fry the onion and celery in the butter until softened.
Stir in the tomato mixture and pour over the chops.

Cover the casserole and cook for a further 45 minutes.

SAUCE FOR SALMON OR TROUT

¼ pint mayonnaise   2 teaspoons finely grated lemon rind
1/8th pint whipped cream   1/8th pint crème fraiche
Squeeze of lemon juice   Salt and pepper
4 tablespoons of fresh chopped mixed herbs, including parsley and chives
Or
4 tablespoons chopped watercress.

This is a cold sauce which can be served with hot or cold fish

SPORTSMANS' CHICKEN (my version)

This is so easy, and very popular with my guests. When they ask for the recipe, I am almost too embarrassed to tell them!!

Per person: 1 Breast of chicken, or chicken joint
          1 tablespoon clear honey
          1 teaspoon whole grain mustard.
          1 tablespoon water

Mix together the honey, mustard and water and pour over the chicken. You can prepare this earlier, and leave the chicken to marinade.
Cook at 170-180 degrees C for 45 minutes, turning 2 or 3 times, but making sure it's skin -side up for the final few minutes.
If you are particularly health conscious, you can use skinless chicken, but make sure that the chicken doesn't dry out in the cooking.

SPICY CHICKEN (4)

Saute 1 finely chopped onion in 1½ oz butter.
Add 1 tablespoon flour, 1 tablespoon curry powder and ¾ pint milk.
Simmer gently until the sauce thickens.
Add 1 teaspoon of each of the following: tomato puree
                                        Mango chutney
                                        Soft brown sugar
Plus the grated rind and juice of 1 orange.
Add 1lb cooked chicken.

Simmer gently for 20 minutes, stirring occasionally to make sure it doesn't stick.

CHICKEN FRICASSEE (4)

A favourite recipe from my college days.

Boil about 1 lb chicken meat, or a whole chicken, gently, until cooked. Pick off the meat, and roughly chop whilst still hot.
Make up to 1 pint of 2/3rds milk and 1/3rd chicken stock.
Make a white sauce using 2oz butter and 2 oz plain flour and the pint of liquid. Season.
Add the hot chicken, and a good squeeze of lemon juice.
Serve with a garnish comprising a baked roll of bacon, baked mushroom, crescent shaped croute and a lemon wedge per person.

BAKED MUSHROOMS A LA MRS. BEETON

In my book, the only way to cook mushrooms - the flavour is superb.
Wash the mushrooms, and remove the stalks.
Place in a baking dish, with a good knob of butter in each cup.
Cook in a hot oven for about 15 minutes.

GILLY'S HUNGARIAN GOULASH (10)

For twelve glorious years, from 1969, I lived and worked in north Hampshire. Social life was fantastic and frenetic, and my friends, and I, went to many dinner parties. This dish was a favourite, especially as it is best if cooked the day before, which made it more practical to hold parties when you were also gainfully employed. We were introduced to this by Gilly - a girl with a great zest for life. Sadly, she died in 2007, so this dish has to be dedicated to her , with a toast of her (and my!) favourite tipple of a gin and tonic!

Put 1lb of dried apricots in a bowl, cover with water, and leave to soak.

Shake 5lb diced steak in 6oz flour. (We had good appetites in those days!)
Melt ½ lb butter in a pan, and brown the steak. Remove and place in a casserole.

Brown 4 large, sliced onions plus 4 cloves of crushed garlic.

Add: 2 tablespoons of caraway seeds
       4 tablespoons of paprika
       2 x 400gm tins of tomatoes
       3 bay leaves
       2 pints of stock
       Salt and pepper.

Return the meat to the sauce and bring up to the boil.

Transfer back to the casserole and cook in the oven at 170 degrees C, for 2 hours.

Remove from the oven, and add the drained apricots. Return to the oven for another hour.

Correctly speaking, one should add ½ pint sour cream at this point, but I prefer not to.

Serve with baked or creamed potatoes, fine beans and a green salad.

BOILED GAMMON

Mother loved ham, and it was an effort to drag her past the bacon shop window! When I was a child, bacon was not sold by the butcher, but in a separate shop. The family have traditionally eaten cold ham for feast day breakfasts (i.e. Christmas, Easter Day and Whit Sunday). I am told that this was so that the maid could attend church early that morning, and would therefore be unable to cook breakfast. Whatever the reason, to start the day with cold ham served with toast and butter is divine! Mother always cooked her ham this way, and if we were having it for a main meal, then vegetables were cooked in the same pot. I suppose this goes back to the days when one cooked in one pot only, over an open fire. It is also not unlike the method of cooking Cawl, the traditional Welsh 'soup'.

Place the gammon in a pan of cold water, and soak overnight, if possible. Change the water, and bring to the boil. Once boiling, throw this water away, and fill the pan, again, with cold water. Bring to the boil, and cook for the required amount of time, depending on the weight of the joint (allow 25 minutes per lb. If you are cooking a whole gammon, reduce the time to 15 minutes per lb.)

If you are planning to serve vegetables with the meat, half an hour before serving, put however many peeled potatoes you need into the pan. Bring back up to the boil, and simmer.
Cut a cabbage into wedges, and put into the pot 15 minutes before the end.

Carefully remove the vegetables, and keep warm.

Remove the ham from the pot, and peel off the rind. I give this to the birds - they love it, especially if there is a little fat attached! Carve the joint.

We always serve this meal with the liquor in which the ham has cooked, but if you prefer, you can serve it with a parsley sauce.

If you leave the remaining liquor to go cold, the fat will rise to the surface and solidify. Skim this off, and you can either keep this to cook with, or, once again, treat the birds.

HAM PIE

In the good old days, we always had a whole gammon at Christmas. As the days progressed, a quantity would be left, which my mother used to turn into a pie.

Line a shallow pie dish with short crust pastry.
Mince the cooked ham, add a pinch of white pepper, a good slug of tomato sauce, a small, finely chopped, onion, and a beaten egg to bind it all together.

Pile into the pastry case, cover with a lid of pastry, and seal the edges.

Bake in a hottish oven, 180 degrees C, for 30-40 minutes.

Serve hot or cold.

STEAK PIE (4)

Nobody could make steak pies like my mum! They were magic, and I try to make them as she did - nearly! She used to cook the steak in a saucepan, but whenever I did it this way, it would always stick. So the change that I have made, is to casserole the meat in the oven. Same result in the quality of the meat, but no burnt pan!

Shake 1½ lb diced stewing steak in a mixture of 1oz plain flour and 1oz bisto powder, plus salt and pepper,

Put into a casserole along with one large chopped onion, and just cover with cold water. Put into a moderate oven, 170 degrees C, for about 2 hours, until the steak is tender.

If you want to add kidney, then add the chopped kidney at the start. I do not like offal, so instead, I add sliced mushrooms after the 2 hours of cooking, giving the cooking an extra 15 minutes.

Spoon the meat into a pie dish, and place a pie funnel in the centre. If you don't have one, try using an inverted egg cup. The reason for this? It stops the pastry from sitting on top of the gravy and going soggy.

Cover the dish with pastry. Either make your own or use a packet of shortcrust pastry (which I prefer), or puff pastry.

Pop into a hot oven, placing the pie dish onto a baking sheet just in case the gravy boils over. Cook for 30-40 minutes until the pastry browns.

LAMB AND MUSHROOM PIE

For a change, substitute diced steak with diced lamb.

Exactly the same procedure.

BOMBAY MEAT BALLS

This recipe was a favourite with my sister in law, Sue, when the children were small and the budget had to stretch! No, boys, I am not including the recipe for Cheese Pudding!!!

2 kidneys
1 onion
½ teasp. Curry powder
Flour to thicken
½ tablesp. Worcester Sauce

1lb sausage meat
½ teasp. mustard powder
½ pint beef stock
1 tablesp. Tomato puree

Form the sausage meat into small balls, and boil gently for 20 minutes.
Chop kidneys and onion finely and lightly fry in a little oil. Add curry and mustard, and then the flour to thicken, followed by the stock and other ingredients.

Add the sausage balls and simmer gently for a few minutes.

Serve with mashed potatoes or boiled rice.

PORK TENDERLOIN WITH CRÈME FRAICHE AND WHOLE GRAIN MUSTARD (2)

Trim 1 tenderloin, and cut into ¼" thick rounds.

Gently saute the pork in 1oz butter , turning once, until cooked through (this doesn't take long.)
You will have to do this in batches, as the meat won't all fit in at once.
Remove all the meat from the pan, and put into the frying pan a good tablespoonful of whole grain mustard. Stir around and add the contents of a small pot of crème fraiche. Once it is bubbling, return the meat to the pan to heat through, and serve.

BACON STEAKS WITH PINEAPPLE (2)

I much prefer bacon steaks to slices of gammon - they don't seem so 'hard', and not so salt. This was a recipe that mother discovered during the 1960s.

Allow 1 or 2 bacon steaks per person.

In the bottom of an oven proof dish, put a layer of chopped onion, and cover with 1/4lb sliced mushrooms.

Lay the bacon steaks on top, and sprinkle with pepper (I do not add salt, as I find that the bacon is salt enough).

Pour the juice from a small tin of pineapple rings over the bacon (I prefer pineapple tinned in its own juice), plus half of the tin of water, and then lay the 4 pineapple rings on top.

Cover with a buttered paper, and put into the oven heated to 180degrees C, for approximately 45 minutes, removing the paper after 30 minutes.

Serve.

MOTHER'S STEAK CASSEROLE (4)

My mother never rated herself as a good cook. She under-estimated herself. True, she was not one to experiment with new ideas, but she produced excellent plain, no-nonsense food. Our diet was very varied , wholesome and tasty. Her casseroles were superb.

Whenever she made one, she would fill a large jam jar with casserole, and I would carry it the couple of miles to my grandmother's home, so that she could enjoy it as well. I only remembered that the other day, when I filled a jar with soup, for Rona!!

1-2 lbs diced stewing or braising steak, depending on how healthy your appetites are. About 1oz each of flour and bisto powder, and 1 teaspoonful mild curry powder, plus salt and pepper.

2 large, sliced onions   3 large carrots   1-2 bay leaves

Brown the onions in a frying pan in a little lard or oil, and put into a casserole.
Peel the carrots, split and cut into approximately 2" fingers, and add to the casserole with the bay leaves.
Put the meat, and the dry ingredients, into a large bag, and shake so that the meat becomes coated.
Put the meat, a few handfuls at a time, into the hot lard, to brown the surface, and spoon into the casserole.
Add a little water to the frying pan, and heat, stirring around to scrape all the lovely sediment off the bottom (assuming that you hav'nt burnt it!). Add to the casserole, and add more water to just cover the meat.

Cover with the lid, and slowly cook it in the oven for about 2 to 3 hours, until the meat is tender.

This dish is even better if served with dumplings!

Mix together 8oz self-raising flour and 2oz suet. Add a pinch of salt and 2 teaspoons of dried mixed herbs.
Mix to a stiff dough with a little cold water.
Place spoonfuls of the dough onto the top of the meat, after the meat has been stewing for 2 hours.
Cover, and cook for a further 30 minutes.
Remove the lid, and cook for a further 10-15 minutes, to crispen the top of the dumplings.

If you like, you can also cook your potatoes in the casserole. Cut the peeled potatoesinto portion size pieces, and add to the casserole for half an hour before serving.

My Parents
Archibald and Glenys Russill

WONDERFUL SUET PUDDINGS

One of the great pleasures of the winter was the addition to the diet of suet puddings. We rarely, if ever, had sweet suet pudds simply because mother didn't like them. Father, given the chance, would have eaten them all the time, and after he died, mother said that the one regret that she had of her marriage was that she hadn't given him these puddings more often!!

They were also a frequent part of my Grandma (Ellen) Russill's repetoire - no doubt because they were a cheap, filling and nutritious way to feed her large family.

DUMPLING WITH ROAST PORK

This is a great Russill favourite. A large dumpling is boiled, whilst the pork is roasting. When a slice of meat is placed on a plate, alongside it is a thin slice of the dumpling. With the wondrously rich gravy that pork produces, the flavour is wonderful. I have never heard of anyone else doing this, and I suspect that when Grandma was a child, in Great Hallingbury in Essex, her mother would have eked out the joint for her large family in this way.
Anyone with qualms, about beef suet and cholesterol, can partly appease your conscience by noting the amount of fat, in the water, that boils out of the dumpling, which is then thrown away!!

8os self-raising flour with a good pinch of salt.
2 oz shredded beef suet
Water to mix the above to a soft dough.
Wrap in a buttered paper, and then in a muslin (you can use an old damask table napkin). Tie the top, and drop your bundle into a pan of boiling water.
Boil for about 2 and half hours.

STEAK AND KIDNEY PUDDING

These were a standard feature of Saturday lunch. Prepared whilst we were having breakfast, mother would then put in on to cook during the morning, enabling her, and us, to go off and do whatever. It takes so little time to prepare, but so much tastier than the short-cut food that people are so often wont to produce these days at the weekend. We would come home half an hour before we needed to eat, just in time to cook the vegetables ,also prepared early morning. The only thing of which you have to be careful is to make sure that the pudding basin is put in a large enough pan, so that plenty of water can be added to prevent all from boiling dry!

We used to find that lining the pudding basin with suet pastry was just too much, so only a top of the pastry was used.

Dice the stewing or braising steak, and put into the basin, along with the kidney.
Sprinkle on flour, salt and pepper, and work the meat around, to coat it. Add a chopped
onion. Cover with water.
Put a 'lid' of suet pastry on the top.
Cover with a circle of greaseproof paper, and then tie a muslin or old napkin, with a
pleat (to allow the pastry to rise) on top.
Lower into a pan of boiling water. When it is boiling again, turn down to a simmer.
Steam for 4 hours, making sure that the pan does not boil dry.

BACON ROLY POLY

Suet Pastry: 4oz self raising flour
1oz shredded beef suet
Pinch of salt
Water to bind

Filling: 4 to 5 rashers streaky bacon, preferably smoked.
1 large onion, finely chopped
A good handful of fresh chopped parsley - the more the better!
White pepper to taste.

Mix the suet pastry, and roll out as thinly as possible, on a well floured table, into a
rectangular shape, about 7" x 10"

Place the chopped bacon, onion and parsley on top, leaving about an inch clear at
the sides, and one short end. Sprinkle with pepper. I do not add salt, as the bacon is
usually salt enough.

Roll up the pudding , from the short end, like a Swiss roll. Fold in the ends to make it
neat and to prevent the filling from falling out.
Wrap in a butter paper, or a piece of greaseproof paper, and then into foil, or muslin,
to make a secure parcel.
Lower into a pan of boiling water and bring to the boil. Turn the heat down, and
simmer for approximately two and a half hours.

Carefully remove from the pan, and place on a warmed plate.

Unwrap, and cut into ½ to 1" slices.

Put some of the liquor in which the pudding was cooked into a gravy boat, and serve

as a sauce.

This will serve 2 healthy appetites or possible three small ones.

Delicious served with creamed potatoes, cabbage or Brussel sprouts.

ROASTING MEAT

Whenever I roast meat or chicken, I always do the same thing as my mother and Welsh grandmother.

Place your prepared meat in a roasting tin, do not add any extra fat, but pour around 1" water.

Roast as usual - the water evaporates, but the steam keeps the meat nice and tender and moist.

If a little water is left, drain off and use in the gravy.

Williams Rowlands, Cwrt y Cwm
1778 - 1859
My Great Great Great Grandfather

My grandparents, Frederick and Elizabeth Chappell,
with their eldest daughter, Freda

STEWED LAMB - aka - CAWL

Hopefully, people have heard of the traditional Welsh dish, called Cawl. This is a clear soup of meat and vegetables, cut roughly, and is a meal in itself. Depending on how well off you were determined how much meat you were able to use. It may only have been a bone. Each day, it was boiled up again, and lasted for several days.
This dish was cooked by my Welsh Grandma Chappell (Elizabeth Morgan, that was.) I now realise that we were in fact eating cawl, but this is a little different, as she added Jap rice (pudding rice). She used neck of lamb, but, traditionally other meat can be used. When I was young, the butcher would chop the meat across the neck, and a not so pleasant side of eating it was to find that you were chewing on a sliver of bone! However, nowadays, it is sold in fillets. No splinters, but a lot more expensive!!!!
Quantities are determined by taste, and how many you are cooking for!

Peel and cut carrots into 1½ " lengths, split and place these at the bottom of your saucepan. Peel a quantity of onions, and place whole, on top of the carrots. Cut the neck fillets in portion size lengths, and lay on top. Add salt and pepper to taste, and just cover with water. Bring to the boil and simmer gently for 2 or more hours, making sure that nothing sticks. Add a good handful of Jap rice, and continue to simmer for another 30 minutes. Peel and cut potatoes into small pieces, and place on the top of the stew to steam for a final 20-30 minutes. No other vegetables required - it is all there!!

Although my grandmother's parents moved to London in 1867, they returned home to Lledrod, every summer. Although he died in 1927, John Morgan 'Holloway' was well remembered in the village until recently, not least of all because he was so tall! One purpose for my great grandmother's visit was to go to Morgans of Pier Street, Aberystwyth, to replenish her collection of bonnets! When they were courting, John would ride, by horse, from Lledrod across the hills to Llaneithyr, near Devil's Bridge, and back again, every Sunday. Such is the motivation of love!

A QUICK SUPPER

Before us children came along to spoil their social life, our parents would sometimes go to the cinema in the neighbouring village of Petts Wood., walking along the footpath that follows the edge of the railway line.
One evening, the star of the film prepared himself a supper, and father couldn't wait to get home to try it out for himself! It became a great favourite.
The ingredients are chopped bacon and sliced onions - quantities to suit yourself. These are gently fried in a frying pan (the bacon will produce its own fat). When cooked through, pour in beaten egg plus a little salt (not too much in case the bacon is salty) and pepper. Stir ir around until the egg is cooked (it will look a bit like scrambled egg.) Serve with a piece of bread. Wonderful!!

ASPARAGUS RISOTTO (2)

250gm Arborio rice
2 bunches of fresh asparagus
1 medium onion, finely chopped
2 tablespoons olive oil
1 litre stock
Fresh parmesan cheese shavings

Heat the oil in a large frying pan and gently fry the onion until soft (but not coloured.)
Add the dry Arborio rice, and stir around for approximately one minute.
Pour in a little stock, and stir.
As the stock 'disappears', keep adding a little more, always stirring. This will take
about ½ hour, and you will finally use up all the stock, and the rice will be cooked.

Meanwhile, trim the asparagus - hold the spears between two fingers and bend. It will
break at the point where it ceases to be edible!
Cook the spears in the microwave until cooked, but still firm. Cut into 1" lengths, and
stir into the cooked rice.
Add black pepper to taste.
Serve with shavings of parmesan cheese.

You could serve smaller portions of the risotto as a 'starter'.

PRANKS AND PRIZES

Do not ask how this got its name - I have absolutely no idea!!

When my father was a teenager, he had a horrendous accident, as a result of which a
chunk of his skull was removed. This was in 1919, before modern anaesthetics and
steel plates! A young Welsh nurse took a shine to him, and nursed him during his 6
week coma, and the family were convinced that it was Tommy's (as she was known)
care that enabled him to survive. Not surprisingly, she became a very welcome visitor
to the family's north London home, and, in the fullness of time, my parents used to
visit Tommy and her husband at Church Stoke. They were introduced to this dish
whilst visiting their farm.
Slice runner beans, and cook as usual, in slightly salted, boiling water.
Meanwhile, chop up some streaky (preferably smoked) bacon, and fry until crisp.
Drain the beans, and serve onto the plate.
Pile the crisp, cooked bacon on to the top, and, oh what a sin!, drizzle the bacon fat
over it all.
Nothing else is needed with this meal.

PEAS AND POTATOES

Another simple dish, and only available when fresh peas are available.
Shell the peas, and cook as usual.
Boil new, waxy potatoes, and serve with the peas with lots of butter, salt and pepper.
Again, nothing else - just enjoy those two flavours on their own!

GOLDEN POTATO BAKE

It is always good to have a few cheap and tasty meals in ones repetoire!
This is just one of those. I have made it using the local Rhydlewis smoked cheese,
which was a great success, but ordinary cheddar will do just fine.

1lb raw potatoes, peeled and thinly sliced.
3 oz grated cheese, plus a little extra for the top.
1 medium onion, finely chopped

Sauce: 1oz margarine   1oz plain flour
¾ pint milk   Salt and pepper

Grease a deep, oven proof dish.

Place a layer of sliced potatoes in the bottom, covered by a layer of cheese and onions.

Repeat the layers, using up all the cheese and onions, ending up with a layer of potato.

Melt the margarine and add the flour.
Slowly add the milk, stirring continuously to prevent sticking and burning.
Bring gently to the boil, and simmer, and stir!, until the sauce thickens.
Season with salt and pepper.

Pour the sauce over the potatoes.

Cover with a butter paper, and cook in a moderate oven, 170 degrees C., for 1 ½
hours.

Uncover, and sprinkle with the remaining cheese.

Return, still uncovered, to the oven for a further ½ hour, until the top is brown and
crisp.

OVEN BOTTOM

Not the most appetising name for a meal, and I assume that it indicates where in the oven it was cooked, because it needs a long slow cook, and in old cookers, that was what you would get, at the bottom!

Despite its name, it is delicious, and another of those excellent, filling but very cheap meals!

Grease a deep, ovenproof dish.

Arrange alternate layers of sliced carrots, onions and potatoes, ending with potato.

Sprinkle with a little salt and pepper, and pour over some stock, so that it comes to half way up the side of the dish.

Cover with a butter paper, and put in the oven (160 degrees C.,) for about 2 hours. Check with a cooking fork to see that the vegetables are cooked through.

Chop up a quantity of streaky bacon, and scatter over the top. Return to the oven, having turned the temperature up to 180 degrees C., for about 30 minutes, until the bacon is cooked and crisp.

Serve - you will not need any other vegetables with this, as it is a complete meal in itself!

I have not given you any quantities for this - you can make this dish as big or small as you like, for one or a dozen. Just adjust the amounts you use to suit you and your family's appetite.

I quite like to put a ½" layer of baked beans at the bottom of the dish, before putting in the vegetables, but that is a matter of taste, and maybe you will think that I do not have any!

A quick tip: If you want to produce this dish a little quicker, then start it off in the microwave. A few minutes, to get it hot, right through, will probably save you about ½ hour in the oven!

The Russill family at Margate
June 1914
Rear: Grandma Ellen, Gladys, Grandpa William, Archibald
Front: Florence 'Eff', Doris

A FEW MORE OF MY FAMILY HISTORY STORIES

I was really concerned that my readers would get bored if I told too many of my stories, but I have been encouraged, by outside forces, to relate a few more!

What I would like to do is to point out to you that you do not have to belong to wealthy, influential families to enable you to have an interesting family, who leave fascinating historical records. Because of the enormous interest in genealogy, the BBC series, 'Who Do You Think You Are', has been very successful, and the personalities featured have often proved this fact to be the case.

So, what has my family left behind them? References in just about every form of record that you can think of!!

My paternal grandfather, William Russill, was born in Lambeth, Surrey, in 1853. The son of a Master Cooper, he went on to become a Master Cooper as well. Under the influence of Keir Hardie, who he knew, he was instrumental in assisting the setting up of the first union for the brewery industry. I have his apprenticeship indentures. He went on to father 14 children, 12 of whom survived to adulthood. On his deathbed, he declared how proud he was that he had seen all his surviving children reach full age. No one liked to tell him that my father, his youngest, was only 20 years old! His paternal grandfather had been a Market Gardener, and his maternal grandfather started life as a Bow Street Runner, ending up as an 'Inspector at Police'.
So, for these men, and their various ancestors, I have seen apprenticeship papers, church and census records, wills, bankruptcy notices (Thomas, the market gardener, became bankrupt in 1859, I suspect because the garden he rented, in Isleworth, was sold for building development.) I have details of the policeman's (William Brown) 'joining-up' papers, and of his career. All of this went on in Surrey, with a few incursions into Middlesex.

Ellen Bird, my paternal grandmother, was born in 1869, in Great Hallingbury, Essex, and she was Williams' second wife, the first having died. I own a lovely sampler which she worked whilst at school - an exercise to help her in her reading, arithmetic and embroidery. All achieved at 8 years of age! All her ancestors were in agriculture. In this family, you can see how comfortably-off yeoman farmers became impoverished by the enclosures of the early 19th century. Here, again, I have been able to trace many Essex branches back to Elizabethan times, with the use of church records and wills. Essex has an amazing archive, with so many records preserved. The early Quarter Session records relates how , in 1705, two of my 6 x great grandfathers, Abraham Owers and John Ruffle, senior, plus John Ruffle, junior, were up before the beak for poaching rabbits. They were, in every other respect, fine upstanding yeoman farmers!!

The Morgan Sisters
back row: Dilys and Annie
Front Row: Frances, Louisa and Elizabeth

Ellen, and her husband, William Russill, produced , amongst their 6 children, two very interesting daughters. Florence, known to us as Eff, was the first female company secretary in the City of London, working for a firm of fur importers, owned by White Russians. I loved visiting the factory, and getting 'lost' amidst thousands of mink pelts. This would horrify people today, but to a little girl, it was heaven. Another daughter, Doris, had a beautiful soprano voice. She and her husband lived in Lagos, Nigeria, for many years, and she was often invited to sing at Government House for various 'notables', including the Prince of Wales (later King Edward VIII and, then, the Duke of Windsor.) His behaviour did not endear him to the worthies of Lagos, apparently! During World War 2, Doris helped run a canteen for servicemen who docked in Lagos. For this she was decorated, and I possess a beautiful African gold brooch presented to her by The West African Rifles, depicting their regimental badge.

And what about my mother's side of the family? Her father, Frederick Chappell, manager of a building firm (his claim to fame: to organise the railing around the top of The Monument in Pudding Lane, to stop people from committing suicide), was born in London, but his family came from Suffolk, where they had resided from at least the 15th century. There are various mentions of the Chappells in the book, but I can also mention that his great grandfather, Nathaniel Hempson, was a peruke maker from Harwich, and I have traced the Hempsons back to the early 1600s. Nathaniel's daughter, Rebecca, married a butcher from Woodbridge, called Tollemache Cole. I have a small diary that Rebecca wrote, as she lay dying from consumption. Already widowed, she was concerned as to the future and well- being of her very young children. It makes sad reading, and finishes a few days before she died, in 1822. Her father-in-law, George Cole, also a butcher, died on his brother's farm, not far from Woodbridge, in 1806. An inquest was held into his death, and I have the witness statements. Yet more intriguing documents that are available to the family historian.

Finally, the Welsh connection (a fitting title given their very close connection to the Welsh Calvinistic Methodist cause!) My maternal grandmother, Elizabeth Morgan, was born in north London, in 1877. Her father, John Morgan, a founding deacon of Sussex Road Chapel, had gone to London, like so many young Cardiganshire men before him, to oversee the arrival of cattle coming up from the family farms in Lledrod, to the London markets, and to run a dairy. The Morgans lived in the Bronant, Lledrod area for several generations, and were fairly unusual, and fortunate, in being landowners, at a time when most farms were owned by the large estates, like Nanteos. John grew up at Llwynmerchgwilim, and they also farmed Ffosgoy, Gorsfawr, and Bronbanadl. One of John's uncles was an Excise officer, and retired to Navy Hall. I believe it is John's great grandfather, another John Morgan, alias John Morgan Walter, who in 1789, found himself in Cardigan gaol for failure to repay a debt of in excess of £400, (now a figure of over £22,000). Sadly, details of his case have not survived, and the only reason that his sojourn in gaol is recorded is that he helped a horse thief, one Daniel Rees of Cellan, to escape by unfastening his leg chains! It is this John who I believe to be the son in law of the Rev. Daniel Rowlands, Llangeitho, the great Apostle of Wales. My great grandmother was Ann Jones of Llaneithyr, near Devil's Bridge. Her mother, Ann , nee Rowlands, used to teach the children in her front room in the 1840s, before they managed to build the chapel at Devils Bridge. She was a great gossip, extracting information from her pupils, and there is a lovely account of her in a 1920s article in the Cambrian News. She was the daughter of William Rowlands, Cwrt y cwm, in Llanychairn, and it was this William that did so much to help many chapels get on their feet. He was one of five remarkable brothers, all born in the second half of the 18th century, in Llanrhystud, and, the younger ones, in Llanfihangel y Creuddyn. Whilst William was so staunchly non-conformist, his brother, Daniel Rowlands, Erwbarfe, Ysbytty Cynfyn was a strong churchman, (he finally retired to one of the big mansions in the Teifi valley.) Abraham became a doctor, looking after the needs of the workers of Crawshaw Bailey in the valleys. Yet another brother farmed in Llanilar, where he also looked after lunatics.

 So, there you have the background to my family, and to many of the people who have been responsible for the following recipes. You can get some idea of the fascinating records that I have come across whilst researching my family history, and, you, no doubt, could do the same!

And, finally, what about myself? I was born in Orpington, in Kent, just after World War 2, and experienced a very happy childhood with my sister Kathryn and brother Richard, marred only by a grim eighteen months when I was twelve, when my only grandmother died (my other grandparents died before I was born,) followed six months later by the tragic death of my father, and then, not many months later, the loss of my culinary mentor, Auntie Doris.

 I left the grammar school in 1964, intending to take up nursing. I very quickly discovered that this was not the career for me. However, my brief six weeks at St. Thomas' Hospital, coincided with the death of Sir Winston Churchill, and us nurses were ushered into the Palace of Westminster for his Lying in State, through a back door, so that we could bypass the many miles of people queuing to pay their respects to this great man.

I then had time to kill before I was able to go the Leicester College of Domestic Science, and landed myself a peach of job, at The Duke of Edinburgh's Award Office, in Westminster. The director was Sir John Hunt, of Mount Everest fame, and I have handled the crampons that went up the mountain on that memorable expedition!! Many fascinating people gave their time to the scheme, and a frequent visitor to the office, who I met, was the war hero, Col. Maurice Buckmaster, who worked so closely with the French resistance. I remember a charming elderly gentleman, no doubt quite different from his persona during the war! Whilst there, I also learnt how to make champagne cocktails!

 I spent three years at college, where I took a course equipping me for management in the hotel and catering industry. I have never planned my life, but have rather let life organise me. Consequently, I have fallen on my feet many times. After leaving college, I went to work at Elvetham Hall, a management conference centre in Hampshire, initially as housekeeper, and then as Manager. Eight years of enormous fun, and some work. My boss, was Hugh Hammersley, who was such an inspiration and delight to work for.

Then I joined the John Lewis Partnership at their Waitrose head office where I stayed for four years, running their staff dining room, feeding in excess of 800 people, twenty four hours a day, seven days of the week! After that, in the early 1980s, I was employed by the Wiltshire Folk Life Society, to set up a café for them in Avebury, (I don't recommend cooking pancakes for over 100 children on Shrove Tuesday.)

From there, I moved down to Dorset, to Parnham House, where my eyes were opened to the delights of modern bespoke furniture, working for the designer, John Makepiece, running the hostel for his woodworking students., and meeting yet more fascinating people.

And, finally, into self-employment, first, from 1985, in Tintern in Monmouthshire, where I had a guest house a stones throw from the Abbey, and right on the edge of the River Wye. A crash course in understanding tides ensued!! The house had been an ancient storage barn for the Abbey, but when it was converted into a dwelling, in the 1960s, the then owners had the good sense to lay four feet of concrete, so one had to climb steps up to the 'ground floor'. On many occasions I was grateful for every inch of those four feet, when the river was in flood - but, the upside was that I had a wondrously fertile garden! Running a guest house does not allow many outside interests unless they are close to home, so I was greatly involved with the little parish church, and spent eight years sitting on the Tintern Community Council. I also learnt how to garden, mine being surrounded by a beautiful eight foot high stone wall. Always interested in local history, I wrote my first book about Tintern, and this raised several thousand pounds for the village church.... So I am hoping for a similar success with this one!

Finally, in 1999, I arrived in Rhydlewis, very lucky to have found the lovely house in which I live. Five hectic months were spent renovating it, and the guest house was ready for business in the New Year of 2000. Once again, local life seems to have embraced me, and I have finally achieved my desire to live in the county of my Cardiganshire ancestors.

EAT YOUR GREENS!

SAUTEED LEEKS

Leeks produce a lot of liquid when cooking, so I never cook them in water.

Wash the leeks thoroughly, and slice very thinly.
Melt a little butter in a saucepan, add the sliced leek with a pinch of salt. Stir around, lower the heat and replace the saucepan lid.

Leave the leeks to 'sweat' until they are cooked - they will need periodic stirring to prevent browning.

Do not over cook - khaki coloured leeks are very un-appetising. Stop cooking whilst they are still a bright green .

On the subject of over cooked vegetables, a good friend of mine, Duncan, now resident in Oz., had a mother who was a little culinary challenged. She would put the cabbage on to boil before she went to chapel. Duncan said that it wasn't until he left home that he discovered that you didn't have to pour the cabbage onto the plate!!

CASSEROLED CARROTS

When I was at catering college, we used to be taught about 'conservative cooking'. No, not catering for the Tories, but cooking without wasting too much energy. In other words, if you are already using the oven for something else, maximise the use of the other shelves.

I hate carrots that have been steamed or boiled, but cooking carrots in the oven produces an excellent flavour.

Peel the carrots and cut into fingers. Put into a small casserole, add salt and pepper to taste, plus a teaspoonful of brown sugar, (or a tablespoonful of honey), and a good knob of butter.
Cover with water, and place in the oven.

Cook for a minimum of 1 hour, but they won't spoil if left for longer. Actually, they taste better if the water nearly evaporates, and the carrots become sticky with the honey and butter.

Drain off the remaining water, and serve.

COURGETTES

If you grow your own courgettes, be prepared for a glut! It's not possible to keep them for too long, and they are difficult to preserve (actually, there are one or two ways, soups and ratatouille freeze really well, and I am told that courgette cake is good, but I have not tried this,) so one has to think of various ways to serve them. They are, of course, an excellent addition to mixed roast vegetables, but try these two recipes:

1.) Slice thinly and put into a Pyrex casserole. Layer with freshly chopped, mixed herbs, salt and pepper, plus a good knob of butter on the top.
Cover and microwave for a few minutes, stirring once or twice. Drain off the 'water' that's produced and serve.

2.) Slice courgettes thinly and layer in a baking dish. Smooth over some crème fraiche and salt and pepper. Cover with a mixture of breadcrumbs and grated cheese.
Pop into a hot oven until the courgettes are cooked and the top crisp and golden.

CREAMED PARSNIPS

Not everyone likes parsnips, but I have won over a number of non-parsnip eaters with this dish. This recipe was given to me by my friend Andrea, who says that she could eat the whole dish for supper! But I warn you, it is rich!

Peel 2 large parsnips, and trim off the end root. Holding the stalk end, coarsely grate, and then discard the stalk.
Melt 2-3ozs butter in a saucepan, and add the grated parsnip. Reduce the heat, and put the lid on the pan, stirring occasionally.
After about 10 minutes, add salt and pepper, plus a good quantity of freshly grated nutmeg (about ½ heaped teaspoonful.)
Pour in ½ pint double cream, and bring gently to the boil.
Turn into an ovenproof serving dish.
Put into a hot oven, for about 30 minutes, until browned.

You can prepare this earlier if required, and then cook it off in the oven when you are ready.

BUTTERED SLICED POTATOES

Par boil whole, peeled potatoes for about 10 minutes.
Slice very thinly, and layer in a greased ovenproof serving dish.
Sprinkle with salt and pepper to taste, and daub generously with butter.
Pop into a hottish oven to finish cooking and to brown.

SALADS

For four years, in the 1980s, I was the hostel manager at the Parnham House School for Designers in Wood , in Dorset. I was responsible for the physical well being of the 20 students!!
Lunch was always a cold collation. It usually comprised of a main dish or cold meats, plus 4 or 5 different salads, bread and fruit. Trying to produce that number of different salads each day was a challenge (so was living with 20 young men).

COLESLAW WITH PINEAPPLE

Make the coleslaw in the usual way, using white cabbage, carrots, onions and mayonnaise.

Add 2 handfuls of sultanas and a small tin of drained pineapple pieces.

Sometimes, I add flaked almonds.

CURRIED POTATO SALAD

Make your potato salad in the usual way, but add a little mild curry powder for a change,

SWEET CORN AND PEPPER SALAD

Take a large tin of sweet corn, and drain.

Stir in a handful of frozen diced mixed peppers (defrosted).

TOMATOES A LA BASQUE

I confess that I have taken, as my inspiration, a recipe from Cordon Bleu books, of the '60s.

Roast 3 red peppers, until the skin is black. Cool in cold water, and peel. De-seed, and slice thinly.
Scald and skin 4 tomatoes, and slice thinly.

Make a dressing of: 1 teaspoonful of tomato puree
1 teaspoonful paprika
1 crushed clove of garlic
½ teaspoonful caster sugar
Salt and black pepper
2 tablespoons red wine vinegar
6 tablespoons of olive oil
Stir the tomatoes and peppers into the dressing.

VINAIGRETTE

One of my aunts, known affectionately as Eff, lived in north London. Her flat was in a block built over a John Lewis department store, called John Barnes -(I was introduced to the delights of shopping with the John Lewis Partnership from a very early age!) As children, my sister, brother and I were each, individually, invited to stay for the weekend - 'A Treat'. At the tender age of 8, I would be put on the train for London, on my own, and my aunt would meet me at Charing Cross. By the time I was 11 years old, I was deemed old enough to cross London, by tube, unaccompanied. How times have changed.

These weekend jaunts were wonderful - we were treated like adults - or so we thought at the time!

Eff was an excellent cook, having learnt her skills from her mother, my Grandma Russill. I wish I had her recipe for tomato soup. It was wonderful, but sadly lost. However, she did teach me how to make a vinaigrette. No bought vinaigrette comes anywhere close to the real thing. I make a large quantity which I keep in the fridge. The oil will solidify, so, when you want to use some, just remember to take it out of the 'fridge a little while before you need it to allow it to get back to room temperature.

Into a large jam jar, with a screw-top lid, put 1 pint of good quality olive oil and 1/3 pint of wine vinegar (these days, we have been introduced to Balsamic vinegar, which I also use.) Add ½ teaspoonful salt, ½ teaspoonful freshly ground black pepper, 1 teaspoonful caster sugar and 1 level teaspoonful mustard powder.

Put the lid back onto the bottle, tightly, and shake vigorously until all the dry ingredients have dissolved.

CUCUMBER SALAD

Peel and very thinly slice a cucumber.
Finely chop a small onion, and put into the same dish as the cucumber.
Add a good handful of sunflower seeds, and pour over a vinaigrette dressing.

This is best left for a couple of hours before using, and will keep very well until the next day.

TOMATO SALAD

Thinly slice tomatoes, and layer into a serving bowl.
Sprinkle with chopped onions and chopped fresh mint.
Pour over a little vinaigrette

SUMPTUOUS SWEETS

CARAMELLE PEACHES

My sister-in-law, Sue, and I have known each other from the age of 5, when we met at the Montclair House Preparatory School. In fact, we went on to grammar school together, as well. Our families became good friends, and the two mothers were a formidable duo!
Sue's parents had a fine peach tree in their garden, and one year the tree went into overdrive and produced masses of fruit. Sue's mum, Josie, was ever up for a culinary challenge, and this was one of her solutions for using up the fruit.

Skin 4 peaches, cut in half and remove the stones. Place 2 peach halves in each of 4 sundae dishes.

In a milk pan, gently heat 1 tablespoon butter, 2 tablespoons milk and one breakfast cup of Demerara sugar. When it reaches boiling point, gently simmer for 7 minutes, stirring with a wooden spoon. Remove from the heat, and beat, still using the wooden spoon, until the sauce begins to thicken.

Pour over the peaches, and allow to cool.
Serve with cream.

HAZELNUT MERINGUE CAKE

This is another of Josie's recipes. She was an adventurous cook, and many a meal started with the words, "Now, this is an experiment….." and it never failed!

6oz shelled hazelnuts
12ozs caster sugar
¾ teaspoon vinegar
½ lb raspberries

5 egg whites
2-3 drops vanilla essence
½ pint double cream
1 tablespoon icing sugar

Bake the nuts in a moderate oven for about 10 minutes. Then remove the husks by rubbing in a clean tea towel. Grind the nuts.
Whisk the egg whites to foaming and add the caster sugar one tablespoon at a time, beating continually until very stiff. Whisk in the vanilla essence and vinegar, and lastly, fold in the prepared nuts using a metal spoon.

Turn into 2 x 9" greased and lined sandwich tins.

Bake 30-40 minutes in a moderate oven, 190 degrees c. Cool slightly, and turn out from the tins.
When completely cool, spread the cream, and then the raspberries, over one cake. Top with the other, and sprinkle with icing sugar before serving.

APPLE AMBER (4)

One of mother's recipes.

Make an apple puree by slicing cooking apples, and to each pound of apples add 2 tablespoons of granulated sugar and the juice of ½ a lemon.
Cover with a buttered paper and saucepan lid, and cook very gently until a pulp, and mash.

To each 2lb. Puree, beat in 1 oz. Butter and 2 egg yolks.
Place in a baking dish.
Whisk 2 egg whites with a pinch of salt and 2 teaspoons caster sugar (of a 4 oz. Quantity), and beat for ½ minute.
Stir in the remainder of the 4 ozs. Sugar with a metal spoon.
Pile onto the apple, and sprinkle with caster sugar.

Bake in the oven at 170 degrees C, for 30 minutes, until the top is crisp and golden.

CHOCOLATE SAUCE

Delicious with vanilla ice cream (which is a passion I have inherited from my mother!)

Melt 4ozs. Plain chocolate with 2 ozs.butter and 1 tablespoon golden syrup.

Pour over the ice cream.

FRESH PINEAPPLE IN BACARDI

Remove the top and base of the pineapple, and cut off the skin, winkling out the little black bits.
Cut into very thin slices (about ¼ " thick).
Dissolve 2oz granulated sugar in ¼ pint water.
When cooled, add ¼ pint Bacardi.
Place 2 good handfuls of sultanas (golden ones, if possible), in the bottom of a pudding basin, and pour over the Bacardi syrup. Arrange the pineapple slices on top, and cover tightly with cling film.

Leave for as long as possible (all day if you can), giving the occasional good shake so that the fruit is doused with the syrup.

Arrange 3-4 slices on a flat dessert plate, and top with a spoonful or two of the syrup and sultanas.
Garnish with a sprig of mint, and serve with single cream.

ORANGES IN BRANDY

Exactly as above, but substitute fresh oranges for the pineapple, and brandy for the rum!

HAZELNUT DACQUOISE

There is a recipe, in the Cordon Bleu series, that I often use, called Apricot Dacquoise. This is a 'gateau' comprising two rounds of meringue, to which ground almonds have been added . After baking, they are sandwiched together with cream and pureed dried apricots. The result is delicious.

I make an alternative version, using hazelnuts and filling the meringue with pureed apple. Just as lovely!

4oz shelled hazelnuts   4 egg whites
8oz caster sugar   Pinch of cream of Tartar.

Filling: 2 large peeled and cored Bramley cooking apples.
2-3 oz granulated sugar
½ pint double cream.

Prepare and cook the apples. When soft, either beat vigorously with a wooden spoon to reduce to a puree, or liquidise. Leave to cool.

Bake the hazelnuts in a moderate oven for 10 minutes. Then remove the husks by rubbing in a clean tea towel. Grind the nuts.

Whisk the egg whites until stiff.
Add 1 tablespoon of caster sugar, and the Cream of Tartar, and continue whisking for 1 minute.
Gently fold in the rest of the sugar, and then, the cooled hazelnuts.

Mark 2 x 6" rounds on baking parchment, with a pencil, keeping them well apart and place on one, or two, baking trays.

Divide the meringue mixture between the two circles, and spread, carefully, to 'fill' the circle.

Bake, at 140 degrees C., for about 1 hour.

The dacquoise is cooked when you can peel away a corner of the paper from under the meringue. If it is still 'sticky'. then cook for a little longer.

Remove from the oven, and leave to cool.

Peel off the paper, and lay one round of meringue ('top' side down) onto a serving dish.

Whip the cream until stiff, and spread ¾ of it over the meringue.
Top with a quantity of the cooled pureed apple, and place the other meringue on top ('top' side up, this time!)

Pipe rosettes with the remaining cream around the edge, and place a hazelnut on each rosette.

Serve with the remaining apple puree and pouring cream.

FRUIT COBBLER

An easy, and delicious pudding.

Put one to one and a half pounds of fruit (apples, blackcurrants, apricots, greengages…)into an ovenproof dish.
Sprinkle with sugar to taste.

Rub 2oz butter into 4oz self raising flour.
Add 1oz caster sugar and bind with 3 tablespoons of single cream.

Roll out to ¼" thick, and cut out rounds, using a 1 ½" circular cutter.

Lay the circles all over the fruit, overlapping, until the fruit is completely covered.

Bake for 20-25 minutes, at 180 degrees C., making sure that the fruit is cooked through,

TRIFLE

Trifle, traditionally, is not made using jelly!!!

Using bought trifle sponges, or homemade sponge, split and spread with jam.
Chop into small pieces, and place, to about 1 ½" depth, in the bottom of your trifle bowl.
If using alcohol, pour a generous splurge of good sherry over the sponge.
Cover with fruit - strawberries or raspberries.

Make up your custard, but not too thick, (even when it has gone cold and set, I like it to be a quite sloppy consistency,) and pour over the top of the fruit.

When the custard has become cold, flood the top with a layer of cream (¼ " to ½" thick).

Decorate with little ratafia biscuits or amaretto biscuits.

I occasionally make raspberry gin.

Once you have finished the gin, one is left with about 1/3 bottle of gin-soaked raspberries. This makes an amazing trifle, if you use these raspberries as your fruit - but you won't need the sherry!!

FRUIT CRUMBLE

Surprisingly, one of the most favourite puddings that I serve to my guests, so it is worth reminding you about it, and it is so easy! I tend to make a large quantity of crumble mix, which I then freeze. That way, you can produce a pudding at the drop of a hat!

6oz plain flour   3oz butter
3oz Demerara sugar

You can use 100% flour if you like.

Rub the butter into the flour, until the mix resembles bread crumbs.
Add the sugar.

Place a good layer of fruit in your ovenproof dish. The old favourite is apple, but because I grow a lot of soft fruit, I also use, blackcurrants or gooseberries, but the real winner is raspberries and/or tayberries.

Sprinkle sugar on top of the fruit, to taste.

Cover with a layer of crumble mix, about ½" thick.

Cook for 30-40 minutes, at 180 degrees C.

To ring the changes, you can make a nutty crumble by adding 3oz chopped nuts to the above crumble recipe.

FRUIT FOOL

Cook your fruit (blackcurrants, gooseberries, apricots etc.) with a little sugar until soft, and puree.
Allow to cool.

Whip double cream until thick.
Gently fold the cold puree into the cream, but stop when the cream becomes too soft.

So that you can enjoy the flavour of the fruit, I put a layer of the puree in the bottom of the serving dish, and then, gently, pile the cream/puree mix on the top.

Serve with shortbread.

WELSH SOUR CREAM TART

This is a fantastic dessert, which I discovered in Sian Llewellyn's book, 'Customs and Cooking from Wales. I have tweaked it a bit!

Imagine a cooked pastry case filled with clotted cream - this is what it's like!!

Place a circle of greaseproof paper in a 7" flan tin, and line the tin with short crust pastry.
Prick the base, and line it with foil or paper, and pour, on top, raw rice or uncooked macaroni, or bread crusts, and bake the flan case 'blind' for 15-20 minutes at 200 degrees C.
About 5 minutes before the end, carefully remove the paper and contents, to enable the surface of the flan to 'dry'.

Remove from the oven, and sprinkle, over the base, 2 tablespoons of granulated sugar (you need the 'crunchy' texture), and 2-3 tablespoons of sultanas.

Sour ½ pint of double cream with the juice of ½ lemon, and spread/pour over the sultanas.

Return to the oven for a further 10 minutes, but be sure to remove the flan before the cream starts to bubble!

Allow to cool before serving - the cream will solidify, just like clotted cream - which, in effect, you have done, because you have 'scalded' the cream.

To ring the changes, substitute the sultanas with fresh raspberries!

CREAM AND YOGHURT BRULEE

Cousin Jane Sharrock was the one to introduce me to this dish, when I stayed with her and Peter at their holiday home near Dartmouth.

Lightly whip double cream and fold into it an equal amount of runny yoghurt (as opposed to 'set' yoghurt.)

Spoon into small ramekin dishes.

Cover the top with a layer of dark brown sugar (about one eighth to one quarter of an inch thick), and leave in the fridge until the sugar has dissolved. Or, 'blast' the sugar under a very hot grill to caramelise the sugar.

Serve chilled.

Maria Chappell
1841 - 1904
My great grandmother
(1865)

GENES
WILL
OUT!

The author, in earlier years

GREAT GRANDMA CHAPPELL'S CHRISTMAS PUDDING

Great Grandma Chappell was, before her marriage, Maria Chappell, and she married her first cousin, William Tollemache Chappell. Their offspring were proof positive that first cousins shouldn't marry. I am not saying that there were huge problems, but eccentricity would probably be a good way of summing up the situation! Their eldest son, Ernest, was an achiever, for he went out to South Africa, where he established the financial structures on which the present day country is based, and he was knighted for his efforts. Sadly, he lost his own fortune through being fleeced by his housekeeper and her husband, the butler, who fled to Scotland and bought a castle!!

The Chappells lived, from the early 1400s, on the borders of Norfolk and Suffolk and they, and the other Suffolk families from whom I am descended, lived comfortable lives as Yeoman farmers, millers, drapers, fellmongers, teachers, and so on. Whilst my Welsh antecedents -the Morgans, Rowlands and Jones - were doing their best to establish Calvinistic Methodism, so my East Anglian ancestors were all stalwarts of the Anglican Church, being churchwardens, parish clerks etc. (the brother of one of the earliest recorded Chappells was a priest and attended Peterhouse Cambridge in the 15thC, and was Chaplain of the university in 1497). George Chappell recorded in the parish register of Stradbroke church, in 1711, that he took his 9 children to church to witness the baptism of the tenth.

Great Grandma Chappell died in 1904, before my mother was born. There has been no way of checking whether this recipe came from her mother, but I do have the recipe written down in Maria's fair hand. The puddings really are delicious, and always very well received! When I was at Parnham House, preparing to make the puddings, some of the staff asked me to make one for them as well. So, I 'bulked- up' the recipe in order to make 30. Some years later, at home, decided that it was time to get cooking, I used the wrong recipe. Once you add two ingredients together, you are committed to the lot!! It took me three days to boil all the puddings, and the house began to resemble a Chinese laundry!

½ lb self-raising flour
½ nutmeg, grated
12 oz fresh breadcrumbs
1lb Demerara sugar
1lb sultanas
4oz mixed peel
1 large cooking apple, peeled and grated
4oz halved glace cherries

1teaspoon salt
1 teaspoon mixed spice
12oz shredded beef suet
lb currants
2lb raisins
2 tablespoons chopped almonds
4oz dried apricots

Mix all of the above together.
Combine with the grated rind and juice of one large lemon, 6 beaten eggs and ¼ pint stout.

Grease your pudding basins, and place a piece of greased paper in the bottom of each. Fill with the mixture.
Put a buttered paper on the top, and then tie on securely, a large muslin or old damask napkin.
Place in saucepans of boiling water for: Large puddings: 6 hours   Medium puddings: 4hours
When you are ready to use them (and these will keep for months) boil again, for 3 hours (large) and 2 hours (medium). I have actually kept a pudding for 2 years - periodically, pour over some brandy to keep it moist.

This quantity will make 2x3pint puddings and 1x2pint puddings, or
1x 3pint, 2x2pint plus 2x½ pint.

BAKED APPLES

Such an easy dish and it deserves being repeated here.
I serve mine in one of 2 ways.

To prepare the cooking apples, preferably Bramleys, choose the size to suit your appetites, one per person.

Cut a line, through the skin, around the 'equator' (this will stop the apple from exploding in your oven!).

Using an apple corer, remove the centre of the apple - I 'attack' it three to four times, making a nice big hole for the filling.

Place in an ovenproof serving dish, and pack the hole with:

    A)   Mincemeat   or
    B)   A mixture of sultanas , and Demerara sugar, with cinnamon to taste.

Press a good sized knob of butter onto the top of each apple, and sprinkle some extra brown sugar, about 1 tablespoon per apple, over the top.

Pour a small amount of water, about ¼ pint, around the apples.

Place in an oven heated to 180 - 200 degrees C., for about ¾ hour. The cut around the apple should have split open about ¼ inch.

WELSH BREAD AND BUTTER PUDDING (4)

I have tried to find out where I discovered this recipe (it was in a book), to no avail, so my apologies to the author concerned.

In an ovenproof dish, put about 2 slices of proper white bread (not the disgusting mass produced stuff), which has had the crusts removed, and cut into ½ " cubes.

Sprinkle over the top about 2 handfuls of sultanas, 1 teaspoonful of cinnamon powder, 2 tablespoons of Demerara sugar and about 2 teaspoonfuls of finely grated orange rind.

Cover with another 2 slices of de-crusted, cubed bread. Cut about 2ozs butter into tiny cubes, and scatter over the top, along with another 2 tablespoons of Demerara sugar.

Pour over a mixture of 1 pint of milk into which has been beaten 4 eggs.

Cook at 180 degrees C., for 30-40 minutes.

SUMMER FRUIT ROULADE

3 large egg whites
6oz caster sugar
1 tablespoon corn flour
2 teaspoons vanilla essence
1 teaspoon white wine vinegar

Filling:
8 oz fresh strawberries
8 oz fresh raspberries
8 oz fresh blackcurrants

And whatever other soft fruits you want to add!
Sugar to taste.   Arrowroot or cornflour.

Very gently stew the fruits, either on the stove, or in the microwave, until the juices
are running, and the sugar is dissolved. Thicken with a little arrowroot or corn flour,
so that the consistency is like soft jam.

Whisk the egg whites until stiff, and then whisk in the sugar, one tablespoon at a time,
until the mixture is stiff and glossy. Gently fold in the corn flour, vanilla and vinegar.

Line a Swiss roll tin (approximately 9"x11") with baking parchment, and spoon the
meringue into it, smoothing over the surface.

Cook in the oven at 140 degrees C., for about 35 minutes.
Remove from the oven, and cover with a clean tea towel, whilst cooling.

Put a sheet of baking paper on the work surface, and cover with a dusting of icing
sugar.
Turn the meringue out, onto this., peeling away the paper that lined the tin.
Spread with ½ pint of stiffly whipped double cream, and 3-4 tablespoons of the cooled
fruit.
Roll up, like a Swiss roll. The surface will crack a little, but use the baking parchment
to help you.
Gently put onto a serving dish.

Put the remaining fruit in a serving bowl, and serve along with the meringue roulade.

MY STEAMED SYRUP PUDDING

I 'invented' this variation of a syrup pudding, when I was at college. I feel that the lemon 'cuts through' the sweetness of the syrup.

Grease a one and a half pint pudding basin, and place a circle of greased paper in the base.

Cream together 4oz caster sugar and 4oz butter.
Beat in 2 eggs, followed by 4oz self-raising flour.
Add the finely grated rind of one lemon.

Pour a generous helping of golden syrup (about 4 tablespoons) into the bottom of the basin, along with a tablespoon of flaked almonds.
Spoon the sponge mixture into the basin.

Lightly place a circle of baking parchment on top, and then tie a large muslin or an old napkin over the top of the basin.
Carefully lower into a pan of boiling water. When it has reached boiling point again, turn the heat down and gently simmer for one to one and a half hours..

Turn out onto a warmed serving dish, and serve with custard and/or pouring cream.

AFTERNOON TEA

The Golden Wedding, July 1917, of John & Ann Morgan, with all their surviving children & spouses, and grand-children, including, in the front row, Megan, Oswald, Eira, Rowland, Glenys, Trevor & Gwen

MAMGU'S SUGAR CAKES

My Welsh great grandmother Ann Morgan, nee Jones, known to us always as Mamgu, left Cardiganshire in the late 1860s, early 1870s with her intended, John Morgan, and went to live in north London. There, John established a Dairy as did so many of his fellow 'Cardies'. They duly married, and raised a large family. John was a founding Deacon of the Welsh Calvinistic Chapel in Sussex Road, Holloway, and was known to all he left behind, in Bronant, as 'John Morgan Holloway'. A very tall man, my mother remembers that he had huge hands which he always thumped, heavily, on the heads of his grandchildren - with affection, I hasten to add. She told me that he used to roll small 'pills' of goose fat and sulphur, and line them up on his dressing table to dry out, before giving them to his grandchildren. When we were children, we were given sulphur tablets to eat - to cleanse our blood, we were told, so perhaps Dadcu's pills were also for this!

My Auntie Meg gave me this recipe of Mamgus'.

Roll out short crust pastry very thin. Sprinkle it with Demerara sugar, and roll up. Flatten the roll slightly, and cut into short lengths, and bake 'til golden and the sugar is oozing out.

An historic footnote: As children, we were told that Mamgu's father, (my great, great grandfather), David Jones, Llaneithyr, was responsible for building one of the bridges at Devil's Bridge. The chasm was crossed by a plank of wood, and David was horrified to find one of his children giving a sibling a 'piggy back' across this plank, during the 1840s. Well, we know that is not so, as the building of the three bridges is well documented, and he had nothing to do with any of them! The Jones', Llaneithyr, are all buried in the church yard of Yspytty Cynfyn, it not being too far from their farm. Taking a walk, one day, beyond the church, I came to Parson's Bridge, which is just upstream from Devil's Bridge. Nowadays it is crossed by a modern, metal bridge - but just supposing that this had replaced a plank.......? A few years ago, in a shop in Tregaron, I chanced upon some postcards - reproductions of prints in the Hafod collection. One of them was labelled 'Parson's Bridge' and was executed in the early 1800s. I examined it closely, and low and behold, the bridge is just a plank of wood. So, was there some truth in the story? I like to think so!
Incidentally, for those of you who are of 'the persuasion', the Morgans, Jones and Rowlands, my numerous Welsh forebears, seem to have witnessed the original deeds of most of the C.M. chapels, between Aberystwyth and Llanrhystud

CHOCOLATE CRUMBLE SLICES

Most families have their favourite recipe for this chocolate slice. This one I found in the recipe book in the fair hand of my sister, Kathryn, dated 1960.

4 oz. Margarine	1 tablespoon syrup
2oz. Caster sugar	1 tablespoon cocoa
18oz. packet digestive biscuits	1 lb plain chocolate

Line a Swiss roll tin with tin foil.

Melt half the chocolate, and spread over the base of the tin. Allow to harden.

Melt all the ingredients, except the biscuits . Add the crunched-up biscuits, and spread the mixture over the hardened layer of chocolate.

Allow to set.

Melt the remaining half of chocolate, and spread over the biscuit base.

When set, turn out of the tin. Peel off the foil, and cut into 32 small squares.

MELTING MOMENTS

Do you remember these biscuits - another favourite component of afternoon tea.

2 ½ oz. Lard	1 ½ oz Margerine
3oz gran. Sugar	1 egg
5oz self-raising flour	1 tsp. Vanilla essence
Porridge oats.	

Cream together the fats and sugar. Beat in the egg, and work in the flour and essence. With wet hands, roll into small balls, the size of a walnut. Coat with rolled oats, flatten slightly, and place on a greased baking tray.

Bake in a moderate oven , 180deg.C, 'til golden brown.

GLENYS'S DUNDEE CAKE
(my mum)

6oz butter	6oz caster sugar
2 beaten eggs	8oz plain flour
1 teaspoonful baking powder	Grated rind of 1 orange and 1 lemon
6oz currants	8oz sultanas
2oz chopped mixed peel	2oz halved glace cherries

Cream together the butter and sugar, and add the beaten egg.

Fold in the flour and baking powder.
Add all the fruit and grated rind.

Line the base and sides of an 8" cake tin (deep).
Fill with the cake mixture.

Smooth over the top with the back of a spoon, dipped in milk, creating a slight well in the centre.
Put circles of almonds on the top.

Put in an oven heated to 170 degrees C., for 2-3 hours, until, when pierced in the centre, with a skewer which comes out 'clean'.

DORIS'S HALF A POUND CAKE!
(my aunt)

Most cooks are familiar with a Pound Cake recipe. This is my aunt's recipe, and she has conveniently halved the quantities, as the original recipe would have made 2!

10ozs Self raising flour	8ozs Sultanas	8ozs Raisins
8ozs Currants	6ozs chopped, mixed peel	8ozs caster sugar
8ozs butter	2ozs ground almonds	4 eggs
½ wine glass of brandy	a 'grate' of nutmeg	pinch of salt

Cream together the butter and sugar. Beat in the eggs.
Fold in the flour and salt.
Stir in all the fruit, nutmeg, ground almonds and brandy.
Line a deep-sided 8" cake tin, and fill with the cake mixture.

Bake in a slow oven, 160 degrees C., for approximately 3 hours, until cooked (test in the centre with a skewer - when it comes out clean, the cake is cooked.)
Cool.

ALMOND SHORTBREAD

The person who really set me on the road of cooking was my Auntie Doris. She lived a very considerable part of her married life in Nigeria, and she and Uncle Alf returned to the U.K. in 1947. I was the youngest of her nephews and nieces, and as they had no children of their own, was very spoilt by them! Every Sunday morning, from the age of about 7, I would get the 61 bus to their house, and spent the morning cooking, returning home in time for lunch! Each week, we would make something different, but at half-term, I would go for the whole day, and make bread. I have never forgotten her description of the dough proving in the bowl, which she likened to the fat belly of a man who had pulled his belt too tight!! She was a fantastic cook, having learnt her skills from her mother.

And now for the shortbread

9oz plain flour   4ozs ground almonds
6ozs butter   2 egg yolks
6ozs caster sugar

Mix all together, and spread onto a greased baking sheet.
Dot with butter, and sprinkle with flaked almonds.
Bake at 180deg.C for 20 minutes.
Cut into pieces while hot, but leave in the tray to cool.

WELSH CAKES

Everyone has their own favourite recipe for Welsh cakes. Personally, I cannot abide currants, so I substitute them with sultanas.

I lb Self raising flour   Pinch salt
10 oz butter   6 oz caster sugar
6 oz sultanas   3 heaped teaspoons powdered cinnamon
1 egg   3 tablespoons milk.

Rub the butter into the flour and salt.
Add the cinnamon, sugar and sultanas.

Bind together with the beaten egg, and approximately 3 tablespoons of milk to make a firm dough.

Roll out on a floured board, to a thickness of not more than ¼ “.
Cut into 2 ½ “ circles using a pastry cutter.
Cook on a hot, buttered griddle for 3-4 minutes each side.

AUNT EIRA'S WELSH CAKES

This recipe was given to me by Aunt Eira, who told me that it was the one used by her mother, Aunt France. It is therefore possible that this was recipe used by her Mamgu, (my great grandmother) Ann Morgan (nee Jones)!

9 oz Self raising flour	3oz butter
3oz caster sugar	3oz mixed dried fruit
1 egg	1 tablespoon of marmalade
Good pinch of mixed spice	Milk

Rub the butter into the flour.
Add the rest of the dry ingredients.
Combine, using the beaten egg, and a little milk, to form a firm dough.

Roll out on a floured board, and cut into circles, as in the previous recipe.

Griddle each side.

A POSTCRIPT

I will, always, associate Welsh Cakes with my late cousin, Eiddwen, from Bronant. As my nephew, Nick, observed after visiting her, "I didn't believe that it was possible to be force fed Welsh cakes" so insistent was she that you had some, and one always came away clutching a brown paper bag of them!
During a conversation with Eiddwen, one day, she just happened to say, 'you do know, don't you, that Handel stayed with the family'. Do you believe a comment like that? Well, all I can say is that the family had lived in Bronant from the early 1700s. The family are connected to The Rev. Daniel Rowlands, Llangeitho who was an associate of Handel, and it is documented that George Frideric visited the Watkin Wynn family in north Wales, so it is more than possible that Rowlands suggested that Handel spend the night with the family as he passed through the village - after all there was a singular lack of places to stay in the 1700s in the area! And why make up a story like that, anyway?!!

BUTTER TARTS (30-40)

Yet another recipe from college days.

Line patty tins, using 1lb of short crust pastry.

Cream together: 3oz butter
1lb granulated butter
4 eggs
1 ¼ lb sultanas

Fill the patty cases with this mixture.

Bake at 180 degrees C., for about 15-20 minutes, until cooked through.

SWISS TARTS (40-50)

Line patty tins with paper cases.

Cream together: ½ lb margarine, 3oz icing sugar, 6oz Self raising flour, 2 oz corn flour or custard powder, and ½ teaspoonful of vanilla essence.

Pipe a circle into the paper cases, leaving a hole in the middle.

Bake for 25 minutes at 170 degrees C.

When cool, pipe a little jam into the centre.

LAZY DAISY CAKE

Beat 2 eggs and add 1 cup of sugar, and 1 teaspoon of vanilla essence.

Beat into that 1 cup of self raising flour, and a pinch of salt.

Line a bread tin with greaseproof paper, and pour the cake mixture into it.

Bake for 30 minutes at 190 degrees C.

Cool.

Mix together 3 tablespoons of melted butter, 5 tablespoons brown sugar, 2 tablespoons milk and ½ cup of desiccated coconut.

Spread over the top of the cooled cake, and grill.
Cool.

My Grandma Russill
Ellen Bird
(1869 - 1941)
taken in 1895

Ellen's brother Bill, with his wife "Aunt
Martha"

ELLEN RUSSILL'S ORANGE MADEIRA CAKE

My paternal grandmother, Ellen Russill (nee Bird), was a Essex girl, from a farming background. She came to London, as a young woman, to be 'Cook' in a household in north London.

Grandpa Russill, a widower, met Ellen at a Sunday afternoon tea party. This was hosted by a friend of his from the Baptist church, who happened to be the housekeeper along with Ellen. Grandpa had already sired eight children, and his poor first wife had died from septicaemia and exhaustion after number eight. With his new wife, Ellen, whom he married in 1895, six more Russills were added to the nest, my father being the youngest. Fortunately, Grandpa's eldest granddaughter, Betty, said he was very good with children, and all the local kids would follow him home from work, like the Pied Piper! Grandpa was a Master Cooper, (like his father before him) having been headhunted by one of the north London breweries. He was an associate of Keir Hardie, and helped establish the first union for brewery workers. Grandpas' grandfather had had a market garden, in Isleworth and his father was reputedly a gardener at Richmond Palace - it's certainly in the genes!. Upto the late 1850s, most of Isleworth was market gardens, until fast-growing London reached out into Middlesex, and all the fields disappeared under houses.

Needless to say, Ellen was a superb cook, and I am only sorry that I don't have more of her recipes. She died before I was born, but she trained her daughters well, and I certainly sampled their cooking! As I have already mentioned, I learnt many of my skills from her daughter , Doris.

4oz butter	4oz caster sugar	6oz self-raising flour
2 eggs	Juice and rind of one orange	

Grease and line a deep-sided, 6" cake tin.

Cream together the butter and sugar.

Beat in the eggs, followed by the flour.

Add the finely grated orange rind, and the juice (if the mixture curdles with this extra liquid, add a little extra flour to absorb it.)

Turn the mixture into the prepared cake tin.

Cook at 180 degrees C., for 1 hour, or until a skewer can be removed 'cleanly'. Ten minutes before the end of cooking, place 3 thin slices of candied peel on the top. This is not the chopped peel that you buy in the supermarket - you will have to 'source' this from a health food shop, or an independent grocer.

Sunday Tea Time at Grandma Chappell's.
Our 'own table'. Judith, Valerie & Richard
(Grandma in the background who always had a lovely handkerchief
hanging from her sleeve)

TOMATO SPREAD

The pace of the modern age means that most children seem to have been denied the joys of a 'bread and butter' tea , (or as my great niece, Katie, calls it - 'a laid out tea').

We enjoyed this meal every day. A plate of bread and butter (cut very thin, of course!), dishes of homemade jam, maybe a pot of Heinz Vegetable Spread, marmite, and cheese. This was followed by cake. On special occasions, and on Sundays, we also had sandwiches and, depending on the time of year, a bowl of watercress or celery.

If we had been very good, or more likely, if Mother had some squashy tomatoes, we had tomato spread.

To ½ lb. Tomatoes you need ¼ lb cheddar cheese, I small chopped onion, and 1 beaten egg.

Melt a knob of butter in a saucepan, and add the peeled and chopped tomato and onion.

When cooked (about 5 minutes - the onion should be transparent but not brown), add the grated cheese and the beaten egg.

Cook gently for 1 to 2 minutes, until thickened, and pour into a basin or your serving dish.

Leave to set.

Serve with bread and butter, but equally good with toast, and, recently, I have enjoyed it on oat cakes. What about that as a party savoury?

CUCUMBER SANDWICHES

My mother's cucumber sandwiches were divine, and a regular part of Sunday afternoon tea.

At sometime during the day, peel the amount of cucumber you wish to use. Still using your potato peeler, peel the cucumber into a bowl. Sprinkle with white pepper, and cover with good malt vinegar. Leave to soak. When you are ready to make your sandwiches, squeeze out the vinegar and spread the cucumber on slices of very thin bread and butter. Top with another slice. Remove the crusts, cut each sandwich into four and arrange on your serving plate. Nephew Nicholas couldn't believe what they were when he first saw these petite savouries, "sandwiches!" he said, "I could inhale those"!

TASTY TITBITS

HOT CHEESE BISCUITS

After Church, on a Sunday evening, we often visited our friends, Esmond and Denise, for coffee. Denise is yet another wonderful cook. The recipe for these biscuits winged its way across the Atlantic from Denise's sister who lives in Canada. These are best eaten straight from the oven.

6oz grated strong cheese	2oz butter
small teaspoon mustard powder	½ breakfast cup of plain flour
Pinch of salt	

Work all the ingredients together into a firm dough, and roll into a sausage about 1 ½ " in diameter.
Chill. (At this stage, the dough freezes really well, if you want to make in advance.)
Cut into ¼" slices, and place well spaced, to allow for spreading, on a baking tray.

Bake at 200 degrees C. for 6-8 minutes.

CHEESE AND WALNUT FINGERS

Yet another recipe from college days!

4oz margarine	8oz plain flour
3oz finely grated cheese	Pinch, each, of salt, pepper and mustard powder
1 egg Marmite	2oz chopped walnuts

Rub the margarine into the dry ingredients.
Add the cheese and bind together with the egg to produce a stiff dough. Divide into two.
Roll out each half of dough into thin squares.
Spread a little marmite onto one square and sprinkle with half of the walnuts.
Place the other square on top, and press down firmly with the rolling pin.
Brush with a little beaten egg, and sprinkle on the remaining chopped walnuts .
Cut into fingers, 3 ½" long by ½" wide.
Transfer to a baking tray, and bake in a moderate oven, 180 degrees C., for 10-15 minutes, until pale brown in colour.

CHEESE DREAMS

Those of you who have not had the pleasure of being part of the Scouting and Guiding movement, have probably also been denied the delight of cheese dreams!

Sandwich sliced cheese between two slices of medium thick, dry bread.
Fry, slowly, in hot butter until golden in colour, and so that the cheese has had time to melt.

Turn once during frying.

HAM AND CHEESE ROLLS

A recipe from my student days. Ideal for finger buffets. Quick and easy!

2 x 8oz packets cream cheese   ½ lb thinly sliced ham

Spread the cream cheese on the ham.
Roll up like a swiss roll, and cut into ½" rounds.

CHEESE FILO PURSES

You can buy something similar ready made, but these are so easy to make - and cheaper too!

Care is needed when using filo pastry, as it dries out so quickly, so follow the instructions on the packet.

"Glue" 2 wafer thin sheets of filo pastry together by brushing with melted butter, and also butter the top surface.
Cut into 4" squares.
Put a little cranberry sauce in the middle of each square, and on top of that some goats cheese or soft blue cheese. Here, in Ceredigion, we have access to some wonderful local cheeses, and I use Perl Las or Pont Gar.
Draw the edges together, like a Dorothy bag, and pinch together. Dab with melted butter.

Bake in a hot oven, 200 degrees C., for about 10 minutes, until golden brown. Watch them - they won't take long.

CHEESE CREAM

One of Denise's recipes!

Equal quantities of grated cheese and butter.
Add salt and pepper to taste, plus chopped herbs including parsley and chives.

Use as a biscuit topping or in sandwiches. It freezes very well.

CHEDDAR CHEESE AND SEED BISCUITS (24)

4oz finely grated cheese	2 heaped tablespoons of plain flour
Pinch of paprika pepper	Mixture of pumpkin seeds, pine nuts and
sunflower seeds	

Combine all the ingredients.
Spoon small amounts onto a baking sheet which has been lined with baking paper.
Space them well apart as they will spread.
Cook as 220degrees C., for 5 minutes, until gold around the edges.

Lift with a spatula onto a cooling tray.

SEEDED OATCAKES

Oatcakes are a traditional biscuit, throughout Great Britain, and in these days of so many people having wheat intolerances, they are an excellent addition to the diet. The oats also help to combat cholesteral!
Normally, one uses dripping, lard or butter to bind the oats together, but I use olive oil.

4oz porridge oats	1 tablespoon of olive oil
Pinch of salt	A pinch of bicarbonate of soda.
Hot water	

A mixture of seeds, e.g. sunflower seeds and pumpkin seeds.

Mix together the dry ingredients , and stir in the olive oil.
Add hot water to produce a firm dough..
Roll out on a board dusted with oatmeal, and cut either into wedges, or using a pastry cutter.
Bake on a hot griddle until the edges turn a golden brown.
Cool.

THAT LITTLE

EXTRA SOMETHING

PICKLED ONIONS - RUSSILL STYLE

My father was never to be found in the kitchen, except for Christmas, when he helped with the washing up, and the rare occasions when my mother was unwell, when he would supervise! Don't get me wrong - he pulled his weight in the house, but cooking was womens' work.

Pickling onions was something different, however. The Russill family are renowned for their love of pickles - my favourite meal during the Christmas festivities was always cold turkey and ham, bubble and squeak and pickles!

So father always pickled the onions, using a recipe of his mothers. The onions are, in my view, the best ever - more to the point, they stay firm, whereas, more often than not, others go soft after a few months.
.

So, the secret recipe is:
Pickling onions, peeled and washed.
Pack into large jam jars.
Put 1 small teaspoonful of mixed pickling spice into each jar.
Fill the jar with good quality brown malt vinegar. I find that brand vinegars
Are very inferior - they seem 'thin'. So I will only use Sarsons.
Cover, but not with a metal lid, as the vinegar will 'eat' through the metal.
Keep for at least 6 weeks before eating.

And what makes this recipe different from other? I do not cover the onions in salt, which some recipes ask you to do, and I do not heat the vinegar and spices.

And, how to peel the onions without crying? Father always did them sitting in the garden, wearing his sun glasses (to keep the onion ' spray' out of your eyes) and smoking his pipe. I do not smoke the pipe, but I do prepare the onions outdoors, and I do wear my sunglasses.

When I was four, I had Scarlet Fever - a notifiable disease in those days. When I returned from the isolation hospital (where I had spent Christmas), my mother took me to convalesce in Worthing, staying with my great aunt Lou. Aunt Lou was happy for me to eat lunch with them, but not my tea - so I was dispatched to the kitchen where I was given my tea by her maid, Margit. During the war, Margit had escaped from Hungary in a cabbage cart. She was intensely loyal to Aunt Lou, but loathed one of Lou's friends - when she visited, Margit would fill the bath with dirty washing to prevent the guest from bathing. Anyway, mother came down to the kitchen to see how I was doing, and was horrified to see this 4 year old tucking into a plate of pickled onions and cheese. I have never looked back, and would not dream of letting September pass without putting quantities of onions down to pickle.

Another observation about Aunt Lou. She, like many of her generation, wore directoire knickers, the legs of which came down to just above the knee. She would tuck her handkerchief into the leg, and I was fascinated, as a little girl, watching the very lady-like way she had of discreetly raising her skirts, and removing her handkerchief!!

GRANDMA CHAPPELL'S GREEN TOMATO PICKLE

Aunt Lou was one of my grandmother's four sisters. They, and their two brothers grew up in north London. All Welsh speaking (even in London grandma had to be taught English when she went to school), their life revolved around the Welsh Calvinistic Methodist chapel in Sussex Road, Holloway. Still a successful chapel with a good membership. My great grandfather was a founding deacon, and the other became Aunt Lou's father-in-law. When Lou died, she bequeathed money to provide a meeting hall in memory of these two men - John Evans and John Morgan (my 'hen dadcu') and her husband, Jack. The architect was Ronald Harrison, husband of Gwen, one of Lous' nieces.

Slice and spread on a large dish, 4lb green tomatoes and 2lb onions. Sprinkle with a tablespoonful of salt, and leave overnight. In the morning, slip into a colander to drain. Put the tomatoes and onions into a saucepan, and add 11/2pts vinegar, 1/2lb sugar, 1/2teaspoonful powdered ginger, 1 teaspoonful white pepper, 2 tablespoons mustard powder and, tied into a small piece of muslin, 1 tablespoon mixed pickling spice. Boil gently for about one hour, until tender, and bottle in clean, dry jam jars.

GREEN TOMATO CHUTNEY

Every Sunday morning, I would take the '61' bus to Scads Hill, walk around the corner to my uncle and aunts' house. Not having any children of her own, (the sacrifice she paid for living with her husband in Nigeria - children did not thrive in the malaria infested conditions, so she chose not to have any), Doris seemed perfectly happy to spend her Sunday morning teaching me how to cook. We would only do one dish. To begin with, it was easy stuff - honeycomb toffee, coconut ice (of a particular virulent green colour!). Then I progressed to scones and Eccles cakes, and so on. At half term, I would go for the whole day, and we would make bread.

During our cooking sessions, Uncle would always be in the garden - always! So where he went in the pouring rain, I have no idea. Perhaps he sheltered in Juniper Lodge, which was his Potting Shed! One Sunday afternoon, we were all visiting them for tea, and my brother, Richard, and I, discovered a large pile of soot by Juniper Lodge. Great fun….until we were discovered, and hauled off to have a bath! Such a lovely garden, full of flowers and vegetables. Doris kept a careful record of all that she harvested, entering the weights in a book. I confess, that's what I do, too!! They grew lots of tomatoes, so come the end of the summer, there were plenty of green tomatoes with which to make chutney.

Both of these recipes were tried and tested by Doris, and the results are excellent.

Green Tomato Chutney - 1

2lb Green Tomatoes	1lb Cooking Apples	1lb Onions
½ oz Mustard Seed	½ oz Pickling Spice	½ teaspoon salt
½ teaspoon Turmeric	1 pint malt vinegar	

Boil all the above together, until all are tender.

Now add: ½ lb Sultanas   ¼ lb stoned raisins   ¾ lb brown sugar
Boil for ¾ hour, and bottle.

Green Tomato Chutney - 2

Mince together:

3lbs Green Tomatoes	2lb Apples	¾ lb Sultanas
2 medium onions		

Add:

1lb Demerara Sugar	1oz Black ground pepper	½ oz Mustard Seed
3 tablespoons salt	1 quart Malt Vinegar	

Boil together for 35 minutes, and bottle.

GRANDMA'S APRICOT JAM

After the end of WW2, Grandma left north London, and came to live near us, in Orpington. We often visited her, and were always allowed to look in the 'Fairy Tin', to see if the 'Little People' had left anything for us! We were allowed one item, a tube of Polo mints or maybe, fruit spangles. When I went to the Grammar School, I passed her house on the way home, and I was still calling in to inspect the tin, as were my school friends as well!

So many memories of her home, but one or two things stand out - the curtain 'petticoat' around the kitchen sink, the huge picture of David Lloyd George hanging in the hall (well, she was a passionate Welsh woman!), and a smell of gas!!

Sunday afternoon tea, with Grandma, was a great treat. We would all be there, my family and my uncle, aunt and cousin Valerie. Occasionally, her sisters would visit. All fine, except when sanctimonious Uncle Jink and Aunt Dil were there. After tea, they would accompany us the church, for Evensong. Thankfully, they sat at the back of the church (we were always at the front.) Jink had an extremely loud singing voice, of which he was inordinately proud - we children were mortified, especially when the vicar glowered in Jink's direction!

Tea comprised bread and butter (of course!), jams and fish paste, cakes and little buttered crempog (pancakes).

Wash 2lb dried apricots ('proper' dried apricots, not the 'no-soaking needed' variety), and pour over 4 quarts (yes, 1 gallon!), of boiling water.
Soak for 48 hours.
Boil slowly for one and a quarter hours, then add 7lb sugar, and continue boiling for one more hour, or until you reach setting point.
Add ½ lb whole, skinned almonds, and pour into warmed, clean jam jars.

AUNT MARTHA'S BLACKCURRANT JAM

Aunt Martha appears on the Essex side of the family tree, she being a sister-in-law of Grandma Russill, (Ellen Bird that was.)

4 ½ lb black currants
7 ½ lb granulated or preserving sugar
3 pints water

Add the fruit to the water, and boil for 20 minutes.
Add the sugar, and boil for a further 15 minutes.
Bottle - this should yield about 13lbs of jam.

LEMON CURD, courtesy of Auntie Doris

2 eggs
¼ lb butter
¼ lb caster sugar
Grated rind and juice of I large lemon

Blend the sugar and butter together to a cream, and beat in the eggs.
Add the lemon juice and grated rind.
Stir over a low heat until the mixture begins to thicken.
Pour into warmed, cleaned jam jars.

ANOTHER BLACKCURRANT JAM

3 lb Blackcurrants   3 pints water

Boil for 20 minutes.

Add 6lb. Granulated sugar.

Boil for a further 10 minutes, until you reach setting point.

Add a walnut-sized piece of butter, to prevent scum from forming.

I seem to harvest so many blackcurrants and gooseberries each year, so I am always looking for something in which to use them.

GREEN GOOSEBERRY JAM

1 ¼ lbs Sugar
1 gill of water (I.e., a quarter of a pint)
1 lb gooseberries

Boil the water and sugar for 20 minutes.

Add the gooseberries, and boil for a further 5 minutes.

AND FINALLY……..

Whilst looking through a recipe book of a late, departed aunt (her own recipe collection), I found the following two recipes - which would you prefer?!!

PICK-ME-UP   Number 1

1 pint Guinness Stout
1 gill of 'black' beer
1 gill rum

Take a wine glass full at a time (!)

PICK-ME-UP   Number 2

1 lb raw beetroot, cut into thin slices
¾ lb brown sugar
1 pint of oatmeal stout (what on earth is that?)

Put sugar on beetroot. Allow to stand, and then strain off the resulting juice.

Mix with the stout.

AND, MY OWN PICK-ME-UP

In the late 1960s, when I was working at the conference centre, Elvetham Hall, Guinness decided to run a course with us.
One of the guys attending told me of this tonic.

½ pint Guinness
I port-sized glass of Port.

I know that Black Velvet is Guinness and champagne, but if I was to describe the drink I have just suggested, it really is like black velvet. Absolutely delicious, and you feel great!!

INDEX OF RECIPIES